FLORIDA MAN

POEMS, REVISITED

TYLER GILLESPIE

BURROW PRESS | ORLANDO, FL

© Tyler Gillespie, 2024
All rights reserved.

First published by Red Flag Press, 2018
Burrow Press Edition, 2024
ISBN: 978-1-941681-31-2
LCCN: 2023950450

Cover Art & Design: Michael Burk
Book Design: Ryan Rivas
Shell Illustations: Richard K. Wetzel, from the cover of *Tide Lines*,
St. Petersburg Shell Club publication, Annual Shell Show, 1973

PRAISE FOR *FLORIDA MAN*

"Gillespie has published an empathetic book of poems." – ***The Washington Post***

"*Florida Man* conveys the scope of Florida beyond the flattened punchlines associated with the collection's eponymous character." – ***The Millions***

"All of it drips with Floridiana." – ***Tampa Bay Times***

"Finishing Tyler Gillespie's *Florida Man*, I felt a sense of having just consumed a layer of the future fossil record of Florida, so simultaneously precise and wide-ranging was Gillespie's natural history of his home… teeming with both physical and mythological lives, creating a confluence of unusual social and ecological forces that are all poised to vanish under saltwater in the near future."
– ***Flyway: Journal of Writing and Environment***

"*Florida Man* is a collection of poems that honors its namesake in every imaginable way. From historical documents to crushing narratives to found poems inspired by Florida's absurd news cycle, from the wildlife to the even wilder people, these poems are an accurate and essential tribute to the Sunshine State's sometimes joyous and sometimes morbid strangeness. Like an alligator, this book clamps down on you with such sheer force that you won't be able to pull away."
– **Ariel Francisco, author of** *A Sinking Ship is still a Ship*

"In Gillespie's excellent *Florida Man*, redemption is wondrously messy and surprising, building empathy that recognizes both the many mistakes and misguided intentions that underlie the headlines and the deep conflict of reconciling a bad reputation and a beloved home."
– **Abigail Beckel, co-founder and publisher of Rose Metal Press**

"Tyler Gillespie's deft journo-poems blaze and sear down the page, shaping the nightmare trope of our national misfit – Florida Man – alongside the various tropes of our misfit nationalism…Native yet wild, the stories these poems tell you will haunt you." – **Geoff Bouvier, author of** *Living Room* **and** *Glass Harmonica*

"This is a rollicking ride through the craziness that erupts all day and night, but Gillespie's poems have as much tenderness as absurdity. This is the side of Florida that only a true poet can illuminate." – **Barbara Hamby, author of** *Bird Odyssey*

I

- **08** Alligator Tears
- **10** Alligator Named Florida's Official State Reptile in 1987, Or, Birth Year
- **11** Cracker Sonnet
- **12** Bush v Gore Election, 2000
- **16** Florida Man
- **18** Year of Headlines on @_FloridaMan Twitter Account (381,000 Followers)
- **24** Taxonomy of Headlines on @_FloridaMan Twitter Account (381,000 Followers)
- **28** Alligator Heart
- **29** A Second-Generation Alligator Wrestler
- **30** Letter from My Uncle, circa 1985

II

- **34** Self-Portrait as Rainwater
- **35** Tampa Queen
- **38** On a Dancefloor in FL
- **39** from Granny Lula's Papers
- **40** Summer Afternoon in FL
- **42** None in the Wild are Native
- **43** Landscape in Which Alligator Fights Python
- **44** Ships Wait Out There All Night
- **47** FL Man Zombie
- **49** Florida Woman Repeatedly Slapped Grandma for Rejecting Facebook Friend Request

III

- **64** from Granny Lula's Papers
- **65** Gator Clan
- **67** Gas Station Gator Head
- **68** White Trash Sonnet
- **69** What Is Up with Florida
- **79** Another Beautiful Day in Paradise
  (from a police ride-along in Pinellas County)
- **84** Drunks & Alligator Poachers
  (from a day at the Pinellas County Courthouse)
- **87** Alligator Mississippiens
- **89** from Granny Lula's Diary
- **90** FLORIDA MAN (a self-portrait)

HEAT ADVISORY

- **92** Florida Man Poems, Extended

—"A Florida man has an alligator farm," says an exchange. By-and-by this item will read: "A farm of alligators has a Florida man."—*N. Y. Advertiser.*

Finds Fiancee After Three-Year Chase

Florida Man Follows Girl of His Choice Around the World.

RADIUM CURES CANCER IN THROAT OF FLORIDA MAN

Announcement Made of Success in Case of A. L. Glass.

MISSING THIRTY YEARS

Florida Man Making Efforts to Find His Father.

Special to The Chattanooga Times.

FOR SALE—No floods, no drouths, no winter, no hot weather on Atlantic coast of Florida. See or write "Florida Man," Ruston Hotel.

COLLECTS $1,000—THEN FAINTS

Names are purposely omitted here. In 1922 a resident of Florida invested $1,000 in a business venture on advice of an associate in New York. Hard times came. The head of the business enterprise died. The Florida man kissed his $1,000 goodbye.

The Florida man, slightly heavy set with stubby graying whiskers, did not appear bitter. "If you don't make ripples you don't get bothered," he said.

I

ALLIGATOR TEARS

Early explorers described crocodile
– gator cousin – as a serpent who

"slay[s] men & eat[s] them

weeping." Same gator tears
thought grief then later called

fake because fierce creatures can show
no weakness. These reptiles owned FL

until 1890s: a railroad brought
tourists to swamp & Felix Fire realized

people would pay good $$$ to see gator moved

off tracks & kept in outhouse: a roadside
attraction. Soon people began to shoot
gators for fun. Let bloody bodies float

down St. John's River. State mythology
hardly ever pretty. In 1960s: American

gator on Endangered Species List because
they'd been hunted too much.

Stabilized in late 80s. Today in FL
about 1.3 million gators, 20 million people.

Now without proper license it's illegal
to hurt or capture them, but laws
say nuisance gator found in house pool

car etc. must be harvested (killed)
if he's over 4 ft long: can never go back

into the wild because he'll eventually find his
way back to that same house pool car etc.

A zoologist recently wanted to see if
mythical gators really cried. He videotaped

captives & fed them "dog biscuit-like food."

His conclusion: they hissed huffed forced
air through sinuses & tear glands emptied

into eyes so that's why. He watched the gators
eat their fake food & cry & cry & cry.

ALLIGATOR NAMED FLORIDA'S OFFICIAL STATE REPTILE IN 1987, OR, BIRTH YEAR

A male gator bellows   heart-stopping roar
to attract females   & claim his territory.

They mate   then he peaces out (as some men
do...). She makes nest: mud & sticks.   Call it

single-mom ingenuity. She lays up to 90 eggs

incubates & waits months   for young to hatch.
If baby cannot break shell on its own   she takes

egg in mouth.   Gently does it herself.   The newborns
instinctively know how to catch   their own food but

they can't yet protect   themselves from predators

so the mother defends her offspring   from a father
who eats everything   – his young included –
if he ever gets hungry   enough to come back.

CRACKER SONNET

In 1917, Granny Lula was born in North Florida.
She used an outhouse as a girl. Cut off chicken
heads. Granny moved south to the west coast.
Gave birth to my grandmother who had mom at 19.

In 1987, mom gave birth to me: fifth generation.
A recent survey showed only 1 out of 3 people
were born here. We're sometimes called crackers,
which in certain parts of the country means: poor white

& racist. But when I was a kid, my Granny took me
to Cracker Suppers where I drank fresh squeezed OJ
& ate collard greens while I listened to her high school
friends who had all stayed in town. Traced themselves

back to early FL cowboys who helped tame the land.
A hard day's work meant a whip crack on their herd.

they were thinking about us." Deb worked elections for years never dreamed a debacle could happen. No legal definition of a valid vote sounds obvious now.

"Clear in rearview mirror." Punch card ballots weren't large optical scans like we have now.

"We humans like scapegoats" she says "somebody to blame. We live for it sometimes."

BUSH V GORE ELECTION, 2000

"Now apparently" comedian Bill Maher joked "ballots in Palm Beach County were extremely confusing because not only did many seniors ask if they had to buy magazines to win but 1,200 accidentally registered as sex offenders."

In June before the 2000 election then-FL Gov Jeb Bush appointed Deborah Clark as Supervisor of Elections. She tells me the 5 weeks after the 2000 election were *interesting*.

"Staff members at our other office" she says "sent flowers to let us know

A lot of people blamed Palm Beach County. Their Supervisor of Elections had submitted the ballot to the local chairmen of both the Democratic and Republican Parties. "They signed off on it," Deb says, "but that wasn't reported." Their Supervisor of Elections Deb says for 2 years after the election needed a police escort because she received death threats.

The whole thing almost destroyed her.

Nothing new about a recount. It was a tight race presidential for all the marbles.

They used what they called a Butterfly ballot layout other states had used it for years.   No voters previously said it confused them.

But there was no county-wide consensus for a valid vote: two corners, three corners, completely removed? All this talk   about hanging chads. Recount: Bush won FL   by 537 votes   out of the near 6 milllion total: 25 electoral votes   meant he won   the   whole damn thing.

FLORIDA MAN

And a man beat his
94-year-old grandma
then ran off with her jewelry
and SUV. Judge set bail
at $77,000, said man cannot
ever contact her (in critical
condition). Week earlier
I had moved home, back in with
my own grandma. At 29,
hadn't lived in Florida
for nearly six years. I heard
of this senior attack on
the six o'clock news.
From our dinner table,
my family – Mom, little
brother, stepdad, grandma –
watched: Invasive man
eating Nile crocodiles
had been found in a FL swamp.
More aggressive than American
Alligators. "They didn't swim
from Africa," a herpetologist
said. "But we don't know how
they got into the wild."
We ate burgers, an inside
picnic: Dishes of potato

salad, baked beans. Another
picture of the grandson flashed
on the screen. I always get
nervous when I find a violent
man attractive. "We'll
obviously follow this story
every step of the way,"
an anchor assured. "You'll get
updates as the case develops."
Weatherman said
it's a record high. Nearby sea
choppy. There's a strong east wind.

YEAR OF HEADLINES ON @_FLORIDAMAN TWITTER ACCOUNT (381,000 FOLLOWERS)

"The Florida Man meme has encompassed black people, Latinos, Jeb Bush, Marco Rubio, and DJ Khaled, but the prototype is still a sunburnt hillbilly."
– John Lingan

Florida Man Seen Jumping Off Bridge With Stolen Sausages Florida Man Arrested For Eating Pancakes in Middle of Crosswalk

Florida Man Sets Fire to Indian-Run Store Because He Thought Owners Were Muslim, They Didn't Have His Favorite Juice

Florid Man Speeds Off in Stolen Car With 9 Baby Parrots Florida Man Meets Up With Nemesis to Settle Online Beef, Dies. Florida Man Suspected

of Stealing Nickelback Drummer's Identity Florida Man With Suspended License Seen Fleeing Traffic Accident on Lawnmower

Florida Man Wipes Feces on Pier to Mark Favorite Fishing Spot Florida Man Claims Dog Shot Girlfriend as She Slept

Florida Man Has to Be Rescued From Garbage Truck After Falling Asleep in Dumpster Florida Man Says He Committed

$7 Billion Bank Fraud Because Jesus Wanted to Make Him
Rich Florida Man Shoots Cat for Looking at Him
"Like He Owned the Place"

Florida Man Tries to Hide From Police in Trash Can
While Dressed as Spongebob Squarepants
Florida Man With Gun in Car Hands

Joint to Cops While Parked in Whole Foods Handicap Spot
Florida Man Wearing Mop on His Head
"Terrifies" Neighbors With Demands For Eggs

Florida Man Calls Police to Report Burglary,
Despite the Fact He Was the One Who
Committed It Naked Florida Man

Breaks Into Neighbor's Kitchen to Look For Sesame
Seeds for Hamburger Florida Man Sets Underwear
on Fire at Starbucks Florida Man Arrested

for Peeing on Trooper's Leg at Disney World
Florida Man Accused of Shooting Cows
Along Turnpike With AR-15

Florida Man Beaten by Ex-Girlfriend For Making Out
With Her Mom Florida Man Holds Up Gas Station
in Drawn-On Beard Florida Man Tries

to Break Into Home With Nothing But Pants on His Arms
Florida Man Pulls BB Gun on Pro Wrestler,
Demands Beer, Gets Rekt

Florida Man Filmed Stealing Dozens of Pigeons
    While Wearing Trash Bag and Bucket on His
        Head Florida Man Crashes Stolen Jeep

Into Cop Car, Goes to Checkers Florida Man
    Found Naked, Covered in Vomit After Allegedly
        Robbing Dollar Store

Florida Man Drives Around Neighborhood Wearing
    Nothing But Electrical Wires Attached to
        His Dick Florida Man in Tutu Breaks Into

Farmer's Market to Consume Fruit and Soda
    Florida Man Dresses 13-Foot Alligator in Novelty
        Top Hat and Sunglasses for Halloween

Florida Man Tries to Leave Strip Club;
    Crashes Into House, Runs Himself Over
        Florida Man Tries to Walk Out of Walmart

with $172 Worth of Steak and Lobster Stuffed Down
    His Pants Florida Man Won't Let Hurricane Get
        in the Way of Screaming "Dicks Out for Harambe"

on Live TV Florida Man Faces Felony Charges for Wrestling,
    Taking Selfie With Baby Alligator
        Florida Man Suspected of Stealing

Naked Donald Trump Statue Florida Man Says He
    Makes Living Scaring Badly Behaved Kids for Money
        Florida Man Arrested for Illegal Ride

on Manatee Naked Florida Man Breaks Into Home,
    Bites Resident, Dies Florida Man Arrested
        for "Shuffleboard Rage" Attack at Senior

Center Florida Man Caught Slapping Man Who Took
Down One of His Campaign Signs Florida Man Dies
"Testing" Bulletproof Vest That Turned Out to Be

Flak Jacket Florida Man Jailed for Golf Cart DUI at Parents'
Retirement Home Armed Florida Man Found Roaming
Around Park Dressed as Tactical Police Dinosaur

Florida Man Caught Performing Oral Sex on Woman
on Beach, Describes Himself as "First Responder"
Florida Man Caught Eating Meth-Soaked

Drawings in Jail Florida Man Arrested for Assaulting His Krystal
Manager With Frozen Hamburger Patty
Florida Man Says He'll Kill Himself if the Coast

Guard Stops Him From "Running" to Bermuda
in Giant Hamster Ball Florida Man Attacks
Fellow Bus Passenger Over "Stinky Yawn"

Police Search for Florida Man Who Broke Into Home to Steal
Sausages, Paper Towels Florida Man Caught
Twerking at Judge Excessive Prank Phone

Calls Lead to Judge Banning Florida Man From Pizza
Florida Man Leaves Prison After Serving Sentence
for Road Rage Death, Dies in Road Rage Incident

Florida Man Attacks Dancing Flamingo at Busch Gardens
Florida Man on Molly Says He Was Waiving Machete
Because He Was "Chasing Ghosts"

Florida Man Released From Jail When Police Realize
"Meth" Was Actually Donut Crumbs
Florida Man Manages to Misspell

"School" on Warning Sign…Twice Florida Man Apparently
Painting Anti-Hillary Messages on Tampa Bay Crabs
Police Tase Florida Man Who Refused to Stop
Playing Pokemon Go Florida Man Steals, Crashes Boat
Belonging to Dentist Who Shot Cecil the Lion
Florida Man Causes Uproar After Opening
City Council Meeting With Satanic Prayer
Florida Man Shoots at Teenagers Hunting Pokemon
Outside His Home Florida Man Fights to Keep
Pizza-Loving Aligator Florida Man Emerges from Bathroom
Covered in Poop, Throws It at Cops
Florida Man Claims He Invented the iPhone
in 1992, Sues Apple for $10 Billion Florida Man Steals
Van so He Can Drive to Waffle House
Florida Man Calls 911 to Complain About
Checkers Order Florida Man Arrested for Punching Swan
Florida Drain Clogged by Massive Motherfucking Alligator
Florida Man Calls 911 to Report Lack of Vodka
Disgruntled Florida Man Uses Front-End Loader to Bury
Boss In Dirt Florida Man Apparently Sees One Giant
Fucking Gator Florida Man Bursts Into Ex's Delivery
Room, Fights Her New Boyfriend as She's Giving Birth
Police Unable to Tow Florida Man's Illegally Parked
Flintstones Car Florida Man Arrested for
Uttering the Words "Erect Penis" at School Board Meeting
Florida Man Wakes Up From Month-Long Coma,
Immediately Demands Taco Bell

Florida Man Swears He Doesn't Regret Tattoo
of Now Old Instagram Logo Florida Man Accidentally
Shoots Himself While on His Way Into Job Interview

at Elementary School Florida Man Shoots Himself,
Doesn't Realize for 3 Days Florida Man Caught Trying to
Smuggle Dead Alligator in Car

Florida Man Tries to Walk Out of Pet Store
With Python Stuffed in Pants Florida Man
Pulls Out Penis on Beach; Runs Into Ocean,

Tries to Swim Away From Police Enterprising Florida Man Makes
Money Belly Dancing in Bikini for People Stuck in
Traffic Florida Man Flings Frozen Animal Carcasses

Around Animal Control Office During Drunk Rampage
With Fire Extinguisher Florida Man Attacks Apartment
Complex Residents After They Told Him to Stop

Having Sex in Their Pool Florida Man Who Tried to "Run" to
Bermuda in Inflatable Bubble Rescued by Coast Guard,
Again Florida Man Arrested For Soliciting Sex

With Dogs on Craigslist Florida Man Gets Tattoo of Donald
Trump's Baby Dick Florida Man Blames Rampage
Through Neighborhood on Too Much Masturbation

TAXONOMY OF HEADLINES ON @_FLORIDAMAN TWITTER ACCOUNT (381,000 FOLLOWERS)

41 detained in Fort Walton Beach
police say   he stole $10.38
worth of summer sausage…

"He then jumped off the bridge
and to the ground." Dunedin:
described white about 30 6 ft. 4in

short blond hair & a light beard.
45 y/o man   in Port St. Lucie
54 Fort Pierce. Lakeland 64 y/o

Lakeland   Orange County
30 Tampa   Jacksonville   25 y/o.
Ormond Beach   69 y/o man

Islamorada 56 "apparently homeless."

Orlando   20 in cop car reportedly
"began to bang head against
partition & tried to choke himself."

32 in St. Pete. Lakeland 64 y/o
Miami Whole Foods   parking lot.

58 y/o Port St. Lucie
Summerfield 27.

Largo "had been smoking spice all day long."

A 59 y/o homeless man.   Dunnellon 28
Coral Springs Holiday described as "heavy-set

white male
in his 30s or 40s" Miami

Jacksonville 44 "stopped by U.S.
Coast Guard & committed
to psychiatric hospital for evaluation

under Florida Mental Health Act

commonly known as the Baker Act."
Alachua County 19 Boynton Beach 56
Orlando 28 Gainesville 50

Pinellas Park Senior Center 81
at shuffleboard court.

Tampa 23
Cocoa-area 19

police said "part of a gaming group"
& "wanted to participate in a flash mob."

Gainesville   Republican
first elected to the Florida House in 2010.

Lake City 29   "bleeding from the mouth."

St. Pete Plant City 42 "recently
been released from prison... for

the killing of 48 y/o [redacted]
in another road rage incident."

Southwest Florida 65 y/o
"Rhode Island transplant in a beat-up
white mask & red polkadot onesie."

McIntosh 19
Orlando 45.
Vero Beach 28

St. Pete 38 y/o Brooklyn, New York native.

Fort Walton Beach
Deltona-area a couple 31 & 26
Orlando 64   Tampa

Marco Island 26   Tallahassee 21
Pensacola "co-founder local chapter of
the Satanic Temple." Fort Myers 25
Crestview 28 Winter Haven 53 Orlando 59

32 Sanford: "standing over [him]
cussing &   laughing about the situation."

Miami 21 took "a fighting stance."
Panama City 28 Deltona 37 Pembroke Park.

Brooksville 57. Tampa
suspect #1: "white male   thin build
in a cheerleading costume

suspect #2: male
(unknown race) in hoodie." Miami 36

38 y/o "who lives
w/ his parents

in the Village of Calumet."
A homeless man 50.

Miami 30.
Panama City 27.
St. Pete 53.

ALLIGATOR HEART

Bag of sugar sized muscle   pumps blood. Most reptiles:
3-chambered heart   but gator 4-chambers like mammals

& birds   which gators used to be millions of years ago

when they were dinosaurs.   Over time wings went
missing: can't fly no more. Alligator males grow

over 12 feet.   Florida record 14 foot 3-1/2 inches

found in Brevard County. His heart   must keep strong.
Animals depend on gator   to stay alive. In dry season

he uses mouth & claws to clear   roots & marsh. Beats

tail & creates mud burrow: a gator hole. Cold-blooded
depression helps him   stay warm. Hole fills with rain

& freshwater drunk   by snakes insects turtles & birds

(long lost gator cousins). Heart makes him   dangerous of course
but maybe under scales – thick set of armor –   he still feels

wings: remembers a time he flew   so free next to clouds.

A SECOND-GENERATION ALLIGATOR WRESTLER

tells me: stand directly in front of the gator   tap   his snoot

he'll open his jaw   he got 80 to 88 teeth   incisors no molars don't chew his food   but he closes with about 3,500 pounds

of pressure if he gets something   in his mouth … don't

let that happen cause he'd go   into death roll consecutive 360s until he could rip off a mouthful   he can swallow

but a gator's eyes   – on outside of his skull – see peripherally

he don't see in front or behind him as long as you don't stick your thumb out you can grab him safe   and tap his mouth

reach underneath tuck   thumb and go under his jawbone

press straight back   he'll close   his jaw   then put a hand over his eyes he'll calm down put tape or rope around his

mouth   secure it   oh boy   you better make sure it's secure.

LETTER FROM MY UNCLE, CIRCA 1985

To my parents: It's hard, i know, to live + believe
to trust + empathize. Don't be afraid of losing me,

I will always be your child. But now i must also find

my happiness, my world is new + growing, unlearn
your fears + tradition. Open your hearts + your minds.

Accept the small hurts + sacrifices for they are all part

of living. Realize my thoughts + different ways for i
cannot suppress my inherent feelings, and through

them I will find happiness which is what you desire

for me / in my own way i will attain your hopes for me
Forever understand me and I will always love you.

Poetry, At Last!

The Tribune has always deplored the lack of real poetry on the subject of Florida. True, we have had dished up to us a mass of stuff with pretensions to the lyric exploitation of the beauties of our State, but the most of it has been of the second-hand variety, the idea borrowed from some cheap rhymester of another region and the execution showing the earmarks of imitation.

What we have long wanted is poetry that is partly fact—poetry based on the living and the everlasting truth—poetry that conveys the spirit of Florida so unmistakably that one may recognize it at a glance.

II

SELF-PORTRAIT AS RAINWATER

Floridians have watched rain fall
on one side of the street & not
the other. A study in luck. Or magic.

Seen steam ghosts rise from pavement
poured in richer neighborhoods.

This is not to say I know anything.

It's to say things sounds deep when
you're high. & I was. Told crystal
meth wasn't as bad as cocaine

& that acid rearranges your brain.
Dragged from pretty rainbow
glass. Didn't like the stuff.

An alcoholic never takes to stone
when all he wants is rainwater.

TAMPA QUEEN

Sixteen but the stolen ID made me 25.
We didn't look alike, just white guys

with buzz cuts, but I got into the gay club
& got drunk with my two teenage friends.

We attended a Southern Baptist school,

which made us sign morality contracts.
Faced expulsion & damnation. A drag
queen came over & gave me a hug.

Tampa's so full of potential.
The city skyline looms impressive.

That night a gay boy so scared of hell
found a little hope on the dance floor.

I later left Tampa bars for an Orlando university.

Missed a city where I knew people
who knew people. I came home
for break & wanted Tampa.

I drove a borrowed car across the bridge.

Bottle of vodka in the back seat
from a guy who knew better.

Sped across the bridge. Hit like 100
to feel the wind. In the club early.

Knew the bartender. He had asked me
to snort crystal meth & fuck in his car.
I politely declined. He still let me drink

for free until fog, let me drink until

blackout

I used to be
the version
in which I didn't say

I could've killed
someone that night

& not every Tampa queen
gets a second chance.

ON A DANCEFLOOR IN FL

for Drew Leinonen

On a Dancefloor in FL
      we wrap arms around

chosen family. DJ plays
      Robyn's "Dancing on My

Own." Yell: This is our song.
      Years before we'd seen Robyn

live in a downtown Orlando club
      when she toured Body Talk

(thank gay god for that album).
      You always took pop so seriously.

A Spice Girls scholar who
      introduced me to Eurovision.

Some people call pop songs
      cheesy, but you understood

them as type of survival – like tonight
      in *stilettos & broken bottles*.

FROM GRANNY LULA'S PAPERS

Mary Ann died & left two little girls: Sue & Secily
who Lum + Dace took to their home & raised.

Lum + Dace were married about ten years before
they had any children of their own. Paley Horne
(a cousin) was selling medicine probably a traveling

"Medicine Man." He talked Dace into taking a medicine

named Viteola. Before too long Dace got pregnant
with Anice (b 1904). Paley nicknamed her Vite from
the medicine & she is still called that by a lot of people.

global warming

a sinkhole mouth

everything you own   )

(eroded & hungry:

oh so very hungry

to eat you &

SUMMER AFTERNOON IN FL

hotter-than-hell

    & oppressive

        white–hot

            mythical

                fever-inducing

NONE IN THE WILD ARE NATIVE

My 65 y/o neighbor Rick plays with the remote-control truck he made. He & his wife have a cat, yippy dog & six birds: three green cheeked parakeets, two lovebirds & one blue-chested Amazon. Parakeets are ancient birds first recorded around 327 BC. They give the sky fire: rose-ringed red-crowned & canary-winged. Rick says he once nursed a wild parrot he found with a broken wing. Bright parrots fly free in my home state, but they're nonnative. FL's one native species, ironically called The Carolina Parakeet, went extinct in 1904. Rick's parrots – a product of the 60s & 70s pet commercialism boom. Those parrots outcompeted natives. "Do you let the birds fly in your house?" I ask & imagine the brood a watercolor in his living room. "No" he says & balances the toy truck. "We don't trust the dog around them."

LANDSCAPE IN WHICH ALLIGATOR FIGHTS PYTHON

(found poem from 2018 WILX newscast)

On camera   python wraps itself
          around alligator on 10th hole

of a golf [course].   Cell phone video
          captured   this moment   in Naples FL.

Golfer says: the python   & gator
          were not moving

the whole time he was at tee box   even though
          python had its head

          inside gator's mouth.
Other golfers saw: gator   drag snake   into water.

Nobody knows what   happened   after, but
     they're assuming   the gator won   that battle.

SHIPS WAIT OUT THERE ALL NIGHT

says Marek, my Fort. Lauderdale
pedicab driver. "It's too dangerous

for them to navigate the port."
He fills his vape & tells me he's from

Poland. Fort Lauderdale is about 45 mins
from Miami. I was born near-Tampa, north

of South FL but not quite Central FL.
It's a big state. I'm here to interview

"Florida Woman Repeatedly Slapped
Grandma for Rejecting Facebook Friend

Request." FL Woman: FL Man's viral
counterpart. S FL, with its ports near

S America, has one of the most diverse
demographics in the country.

I want to ask Marek why he moved
to FL. Instead, we talk about birds.

"You know the small, common kind," he says.
"A sparrow," I respond.

Marek drives me past bars: Elbo Room
& Drunken Taco. Tattoo places & t-shirt

shops. In a window, a Confederate flag
hangs next to Marilyn Monroe's face.

Earlier in the year C FL groups held
a rally. A reported 2,000 vehicles

supported the Confederate flag in
the "Florida Southern Pride Ride."

Most people don't call FL the South,
but some Floridians, like my grandmother,

consider themselves Southern.
I grew up eating collards

hearing outhouse stories & going
to cracker dinners. I've never known

if I'm a "real Southerner," and, if so,
what that even means. People at the rally

wanted the Confederate flag to continue
to fly in front of a government building.

I saw the flag as a symbol of our country's racist
history, but in a box at my mom's place:

a baby bib with my name stitched below
the Confederate flag. My grandpa, from Pennsylvania,

had bought it for me. He used racial slurs
& said stuff like California is full of fruits

& nuts & he wasn't referring to agriculture.
Marek pulls out his phone, uses Google.

"Yes," he says. "My last name translates to
sparrow." He drops me off. I walk past

a t-shirt with Confederate flag & the words:
Don't Hide Your Southern Pride.

At another touristy store, a Confederate Flag
Towel washed in fluorescent light. I want to ask

about Southern Pride, but it's too late. The store
is closed. There's no one to give me an answer.

FL MAN ZOMBIE

"Flakka is big here," a woman tells me.

    We're near Miami, a port city perfect place for new designer street drugs.

    Because of the drug economy: major gang wars happen in port cities. New drugs –
    like flakka – get popular then gradually migrate north. Or they don't & stay

    a local issue. "I've only heard flakka used here," the woman says, "unless
    the media isn't reporting it." Flakka

is usually some mix of bath salts +

    crack. Bath salts, reportedly, caused the Zombie Miami man to chew off
    that guy's face a few years ago. I'm told

flakka is like $3 a hit & gets you fuuuu
    uuuuuucked up. "It warms your body to like 107 degrees," the woman says.

    "It can melt your brain's prefrontal lobe."

Dozens of reported deaths in Florida
due to flakka.

"People get really hooked,"
she tells me. "& they can't ever leave."

FLORIDA WOMAN REPEATEDLY SLAPPED GRANDMA FOR REJECTING FACEBOOK FRIEND REQUEST

According to a *DailyMail* report   drunk Rachel Hayes at grandma's house

                                opened door   3:40 AM entered with a barrage of slaps   didn't stop   didn't stop.

The 27-year old   arrested: felony battery of elderly
                            woman   repeatedly hit her
      for (sic) in home   not accepting   Facebook friend request.

"It was humiliating," says Rachel.
       "It didn't even happen because of Facebook."

                            *

On Dec. 17th, 2014: Rachel's grandma   invited her
    & her 5 year-old son

over for dinner.   Night started off fine grandmother made favorite dish
                    (salmon burgers)

Then   things took headline-worthy turn.

*

Rachel & I were both born in 1987 & grew up in Pinellas County,
               which inspired
             2012's *Spring Breakers*.

In the movie, James Franco sported iconic   FL tats: gun
                    state outline &   area code –
   everything   I considered   cool as a teen.

*

               Nancy Grace called Rachel an unfit
        mother.
    "It bothered me she could be so negative
    & nasty," she says.

                   "I knew her opinion
would sway other people."

Rachel's' coworker – who didn't like her – found
   her blank stare mugshot
           called her   Facebook grandma beater.

           "I didn't want to show my face
       anywhere."

She moved to Fort Lauderdale
       hometown of American   spring break.

Swim teams traveled   to Florida's first Olympic sized
pool.   Post-WWII
       Elvis hip shakes   then
MTV hit the beach in 80s & it became

                    wet t-shirt contests   & keg parties.

It has since died down.   Visitors mostly Europeans
gay men
                    & those who want the past
    to remain the past.

                    *

Fort Lauderdale sandwich shop's   a prime spot
                on A1A.   This state road hugs
        Atlantic Ocean.

                Man in khaki shorts & flip flops gets
    rowdy
in sandwich shop   where Rachel works.
                    Man drunk-slurs
                        you took my money

to friend   in Philadelphia Eagles jersey
    unlit cigarette hangs from lips.

            A couple argues over directions
if turnpike – the nation's third busiest toll road – runs west.
        to the Keys

    It doesn't.

"Do you want me
to drive home?" the woman asks him.

"I can only tell if you're drunk
            when you start doing crazy shit."

Rachel had been lead server at   a nice restaurant
on Clearwater Beach.
   Calls this sandwich job humbling
                        but likes it well enough.

She fills soda glasses.   Customers ask
    about her Monroe   lip piercing that mimics Marilyn's beauty
mark.

Glitter nails   pink & teal hair.
She'll work 50 hours this week.

Shifts   midnight to 6AM.

                    *

The next day: halfway house.
        We sit on a porch.

    Rachel lights a cigarette.
            She never had the best relationship
with her grandmother.
                They didn't see
    eye-to-eye.

Rachel's Facebook name "Rachel Freakin Hayes"
    had upset her grandma.

  "You're embarrassing," grandma said at dinner.

"I'm not putting you
on Facebook with a name like that."

"I decided to go home" Rachel says.
"My grandma told me
        'You've been drinking
     you don't need to take your son
        anywhere."

Because of a previous DUI   Rachel couldn't drive
        so she planned to call a cab.

"I pushed my grandma off him.
  I was like give me my son."

As Rachel tells it   her grandmother
   "about 6ft 1in and very German"

went on the offensive
"dragged me out the door & locked the door
        with my son inside."

Rachel   left a red mark
     on her grandmother's face.

"I'm not saying
                it was the right thing to do,"
    her mother later tells me

"but Rachel   could have just been flailing

      her hands   trying to get away from her.
She didn't batter   my mother."

Rachel left the house.   Police showed up
      around 3 AM said
                grandma called.

    "We're here to arrest you."

The next morning Rachel logged
      onto Facebook
saw
     her mugshot   on international websites.

"I never ever thought   anything like that
would happen to me," she says.

           "It all started from whatever this officer
           put in a police report."

                    *

Florida's law: broad
        presumption of openness in public record laws

  "Government in the sunshine,"
says Catherine Cameron
     professor
  at Florida's oldest law school.

 Journalists & bloggers
— anyone, really —
     can get unrestricted access to
police reports
  then turn them
  into click-bait headlines
with disclaimers such as

  "alleged"
  or
"reports say."

"When you're in the moment" Cameron tells me
 "you got to get a story out."

 Professor Cameron
grew up in Pinellas County
  like Rachel
 & I did

& explained
most states have stricter public record laws.
If a reporter in New York wanted

to do an Iowa Man story

             he'd need to call a reporter in Iowa

— a citizen of the state —

   and ask him to get access to it.

            Florida's public record laws
help us keep tabs
    on government officials

& they're also a big reason
              why Florida Man thrives:

 it's easy to get
       access to him
       to make him
 a headline.

"It's a cultural phenomenon that we don't
 recognize these are real people," says Cameron.

"Infotainment made us all forget   this
           is not an actor but a human being & a life."

                        *

At 18   I'd been arrested

                       first semester of college.
My headline   thankfully
     never printed
              might have gone something like

"Florida Man
      Drinks Too Much

Drives
            Flees

            Gets Arrested in Mall
Parking Lot."

                        *

Rachel never saw   the arrest affidavit
cited

            by media outlets.
            I wanted to read exact wording

                        that lead to
viral "Granny Beater"

headlines.

On county clerk's website
            type in name
                        or case number

Order Documents!
            Request Now!
        Including Certified!
Click Here!

  Def is granddaughter of victim
  & did live together for short time
  when granddaughter infant.
  This evening they got
  into an argument   b/c vic
  would not accept   def's
  Facebook request. Def slapped
  victim multiple times   on face
  w/out the vic's permission.
  The victim is 72 years old.
  Bond action   if any $10,000.

*

Soon after her headline
  Rachel boarded
 the Greyhound bus   to Fort Lauderdale

to disappear

    & now almost a full
 year later   she sits   in front of me.

Says it was
 the best decision of her life.
The felony charge   of "elder abuse"
   from that fateful

   family dinner   long dropped.
A judge never even saw the case.

"They didn't have enough evidence" Rachel says.
    "It's not like I hit   or punched her
to leave marks."

      At this all-female sober house
  residents stick to rules   abide by a curfew
pay rent
              complete chores attend meetings

submit to drug tests
    & maintain a job
"it's no bullshit."

Most residents share a room   like dorm life.

On the screened-in porch   an air conditioning
unit hums.
                    A pot   of Venus fly traps
    carnivorous plants that love humidity

sits on a windowsill.
Rachel lights a cigarette   says her life is better
  now
              than she thought it'd ever be.
"I had a fall from grace" she says.
                        "My boyfriend was cute
our bills were getting paid."

As a server on Clearwater Beach
she had easily made about $50,000 a year.

She was once caught up in FL vacation lifestyle
full of rum runners
      & piña coladas.

"Think about it" she says.   "Say you live in Alabama
& you work all year   just to have

   one week in Florida.
There's drinking   there's partying.

     We don't ever have to do that.
     We don't ever have to work that

   whole year to get this Florida life."

  Rachel's constant Spring Break
    warped her sense of reality.

"I think being born in Florida," she says,
"is almost like being born
   into a royal family.   You may take it for granted

& be real fucked up because of it."

            *

Rachel & I walk through
      the halfway house's courtyard.

A cat named Sylvester scurries by us.

        He lives here
somewhat secretly
in one of the apartments.

Rachel completed community service   through
       maintenance of the grounds.
"I planted all these,"

she says   points to small bushes.   "I tried to water
this whole side.

                I wanted it to look nice."

            Throughout everything
she never deleted her Facebook account.

                But she did remove
      the Freakin from her name.
"If you would have told me

this would be my life"
Rachel wrote in a recent Facebook post

"I dunno lol I would have probably tried to fight you…

Now I'm able to share my story
            with the world
         without embarrassment."

CAPTURE OF A DESPERADO.

A Florida Man Charged with Five Murders and with a Price on His Head Finally Lodged in Jail.

JACKSONVILLE, Fla., April 8.—[Special.]—

WHIPPED BY WOMEN.

Rawhides Applied to a Florida Man Who Beat His Wife.

BIGAMIST ARRESTED

Florida Man Said to Have Three Living Wives.

Florida Man Bound Over On Prohibition Charge

Florida Man Arrested as He Leaves Jail

Return of Florida Man In City Death Uncertain

Drunken, naked man fired weapons, police say

KEY LARGO, Fla. — Authorities say a naked drunk Florida man wanted to know if his .45-caliber gun and shotgun worked, so he fired them into the air.

III

FROM GRANNY LULA'S PAPERS

James B. Horne's ancestors came from Ireland. When his first wife died he later married Ann then that was his second family. Ann was a descendant of John Quincy Adams. James Horne was 72 years old when his youngest child (aunt Hettie) was born.

GATOR CLAN

Before a South Florida tribal pow wow
Billy Walker says   alligator wrestling

started with his people.   Mid-19th century

the US forced   Seminoles & Miccosukee
from North Florida   to an Everglades
thought uninhabitable.   They adapted land

hunted alligators to eat. Four generations
lived in camp of huts.   They cooked on high

ground to protect   from mosquitoes.
Elders & young men caught turtles   & gators

kept them in pit for food   then traded hides
in coastal areas.   Gator still moved like a lizard

with its tail cut off.   "They said if you eat

too much of it like that   your muscles will throb"
says Walker, "so we asked permission from gator

clan to kill it."   Clans: mother's side carried by sons.

"After the Wars, we went down to eight
in the US." Panther   otter   bear   deer

bird   snake   & Big Town, but alligator

clan got lost to Wars.   "My grandpa told me

the settler   – the tourist – went by the village
& saw him messing   with the gator." Tourists
thought he was wrestling the gator, which he

wasn't.   "It changed our world" says Walker.
"The tourists started to throw money at us."

GAS STATION GATOR HEAD

Gators farmed   to buyer's specific size.   Watch band
small hides, tight pattern.   Couch makers want seat covers.
People eat the meat, but the head: a spare part   biological waste.
"We take something   that was garbage & turn it into

a highly desirable souvenir."   Replace eyes with marbles.
Own everything   he's' seen. Florida Fish & Wildlife
Commission forbids taxidermy   of baby gators that depict
an unnatural position: stands like a boy   or gives a wave

to the crowd. Severed heads, though, are fine.   Authentic:
soaked in formaldehyde for fresh swamp look.   A polyurethane
coat. In Kissimmee $25 for large $12 gets cute size to hold
& look alive   look alive look alive. Rows & rows of heads –

babies   adults – line gas stations & gift shops in FL:
a wild thing now trapped   & sold   as a tourist imagination.

WHITE TRASH SONNET

My grandmother tells me   white trash is obvious:
they beat their wives   drink up all their money

& are just plain lazy.   It's mostly men.

They marry blue collar women.   Poor white trash
is different.   They're uncouth.   Rich people can
be poor white trash   if they don't vote or keep

their word.   A poor white trash man can be hard
working   but once he gets home – that's woman's work.

Then you have your poor   working class & blue collar
like our family has always been.   Difference between the two

is education: blue collar take more classes. Most of them
stay blue collar. Hard to work your way out of it.

WHAT IS UP WITH FLORIDA

my of-town friend
texts me

then writes:

"A girl killed
herself live
on Facebook."

                        [According to NBC
                              a 14 year-old

                        on Facebook Live...

                              used a headscarf
                                as a noose.]

I've moved back home
into my childhood bedroom

where I'd dreamed
so often   of a different
view.

"There is something
inherently morbid,"

my friend continues

"about that
state."

*

& months later
it's summer.

Across town
a different girl

stands
feet on edge.
Wants to fly

but can't.
It's so much

higher up there
than the 8-year-old thought.

She's one
of my shyest campers.

Kids chant
her name & she

bursts into tears.

Lifeguard says
jump

or climb
back down.

I wait

at the bottom
of the ladder.

She walks by

my outstretched
arms.

Won't accept
a hug.

                    *

& I'm 6 or 7
or 8 years old

at the beach

with my mom
& her friend's

daughter

Amy: pinches

a Cheeto
between her thumb
& pointer finger

                                        to feed seagulls
                                  [Florida's state bird
                                   the mockingbird.

                                  But I would have
                                      believed it
                                      the seagull]

whose confidence I mistook
for desperation

                        [or even   flamingos
                               in the Sun
                               shine State]

but those seagulls

descended
on Amy & me

& some mistakes
you only need to make

once.

                *

Decades later
I sit

in a doctor's office.
My grandma

suffers from COPD,

a 40-year marriage
to a smoker

although she never smoked.

I turn
my attention
to the TV

suspended above stacks
of *People*

& *US Weekly*.

The anchor's
report: Florida Man
charged
with three counts
of sexual battery
on a 15-year-old student.

These FL teacher stories
seem
so frequent.

         [In 2004
         Deborah LaFave

      made national headlines

            arrested

     for performing oral sex
      on one of her middle

         school students.

         LaFave's lawyer
         said she was too

           pretty for jail

      argued: "To place Debbie

into a
penitentiary...

is like putting
a piece
of raw meat

in with the lions."

(Donald Trump

once commented
on a talk radio show

that LaFave was "not
bad

looking").

At the time
of LaFave's arrest
I was

a high school
junior

not much older
than
the victim.]

The victim

in this case told
deputies she

performed oral sex
on her teacher

twice at school
minutes after the final

bell. Florida man
told the victim

he felt guilty
because of his wife's
current

pregnancy.

When detectives arrested
him

he, reportedly, confessed.

Said he suffered
from PTSD.
Drank to cope.

A Google search
of the 34-year-old
former marine

turns up:

We'd both
been born
in a similar part
of the state.

We'd both
attended
a Christian
elementary school.

From the about me
section on his teacher's page:

He had not
been "sure what [he]

wanted
to do with [his]

life" so he followed
in his mother's footsteps
to become a teacher.

He moved back to FL
after active duty

to start a family &
to finally have

his "happily ever after."

                    *

So approach
the gator quietly.

Gator head: mostly bone

shots deflect
& bounce off.

Aim at their legs
or softer areas.

Won't need to look far.

Large adult gators:
territorial.

They tend to stay
confined to home range.

*

Because some of us

possess
a pathological
need

to explain ourselves.

An attempt at healing.
Maybe.

But it could just be
a waste of time.

Reasons I've heard
why

weird shit happens in FL:

money

                                [both the excess
                                  & lack of]

weather
            the laws

        mythology
marketing

&
Walt Disney.

A country full of people

who would spend their last chance
                        on a dream.
            A plot.
Their happing ending.

ANOTHER BEAUTIFUL DAY IN PARADISE (FROM A POLICE OFFICER RIDE-ALONG IN PINELLAS COUNTY)

Officer says: white guy
told me

he'd kill the black man

who slept with his ex-wife
& a few weeks later

he did just that.

I sip coffee in front
of armory with guns on back wall.

Officer of twelve years
describes himself as

"little Asian dude
with a Southern accent."

He works in a rough part of town
he calls the hood

because he wants to make a difference.

Says people here are
socioeconomically trapped.

Parents: working class.

They're just trying to make
sure their kids don't go to prison

or end up in a body bag.

We ride around. Get calls:

homeless on railroad tracks
report of man doing whip its
in his car a possible DWI

another man messed up
on spice – basically potpourri once
sold in convenience stores

& now illegal.

Born in Georgia
Officer moved
to Tennessee
then FL for his third marriage.

He calls women *momma*

drinks Mountain Dew
& chain smokes
Marlboro Reds or his code

"sees a man about a dog"
his code to take a break

since he can't
smoke in front of citizens.

When someone asks
how his day's going

says	*it's another
beautiful day in paradise*

without any irony.

He doesn't like richer
neighborhoods

calling to complain. The cat scratched
new BMW. Do something about it.

A man wants
to kill himself

& we're there.

I'm not allowed in the room.

As he sobs
man's twin sister peels
potatoes in the kitchen.

Sea foam bathroom walls & cheetah rug.

Man voluntarily gets in back
of cop car for crisis center

so it's not a Baker Act.

If he would have kicked
& screamed he'd go

72 hours for observation.

The officer can't give me his opinion
on certain things though he
would if he could.   Journalists

just like to "twist things"
& his department won't
let him comment.

But he hates bad officers:
ruins it for everybody.

"People only see a little
of the video on social media

& nobody reports on the good stuff."

I tell him that's not news.

He agrees.
Says: you can't
ever forget the sound

of bullets whizzing
past you.

Dispatch: two men
in black masks

robbed a house
they're on foot   rifles in hand.
Adrenaline rushes.

Stay in car.

Dogs sniff
strongest scent.

At the end of his
shift we stand in a deserted

lot near midnight.
He tells me an opinion
off the record.

& says

don't bring the monkey
home from work

& by this he means   stress would kill
him if he let it

& he almost did.

When he was younger:
a mother beat her kids.

Didn't want to arrest this mother
in front of her kids so he let her kiss

them goodbye.

She whispered   "you killed me"
in her son's ear.

& as much as he tried

he could never sleep
the same after that.

DRUNKS & ALLIGATOR POACHERS (FROM A DAY AT THE PINELLAS COUNTY COURTHOUSE)

In FL   anyone can
go in & out of court

rooms at will.

I sit on a bench
at 49th street Courthouse

where they keep archives
of police reports: mine
& Rachel's are here, too.

"I hate this place"
a woman tells me.

She's tan with a smoker's cough

waits

outside mediation
for her grandson's parents.

"He knew something
was wrong. He kissed my cheek
& forehead last night."

Fourth floor: felonies.
Courtroom 10: drugs.

"Are you here
for jury duty?"
she asks me.

Tell her no.
Didn't pick me the time I went.

"I couldn't either"
she says.
"I knew the guy.

Small town.
He got caught poaching
alligators."

Tells me she used
to have a permit to hunt gators.

Got one for her bus driver
friend

so friend & husband
could have more tags.

"They asked me to go
out with them," she says

"but that's not my thing."

We say goodbye
as she walks into a courtroom.

In different courtroom:
six-member jury trial
for 32-year-old man's DUI

charge. He'd been pulled over
near my childhood home.

Lawyer plays video.
Man from New York told

walk heel to toe
a straight line

stand

on one leg. I did same
field sobriety test in 2005.

& on video the man
in backseat of cop car

says "I'm sorry"

as he hiccups
& hiccups.

"I should
have known better.
I just wanted to get home."

ALLIGATOR MISSISSIPPIENS

Formal like when mom calls   your full
name & you know   she means business.

Or father.   Because dad seems too familiar
for a man who left   when you were two.

Alligators don't have vocal cords: suck
air in lungs   blow out deep intermittent

roars   to both attract mates & warn off

other males.   & that's why you haven't
answered his calls.   Can't tell a difference

in this sound.   A charming man will skin

you alive   & you'll smile when you buy
your hide from him.   & by this I mean

my father gave me   my first hard drink.
I was 15 in Kentucky Elks Lodge   his second

wedding.   Later he moved back to FL
& I'd pick him up   from the nearby trailer

park & drive him   to buy high school
liquor.   He should have known better.

We have the same   cold blood. But I can only
be so mad at a man whose nature   is to bite.
Predators – adult males included – destroy

about a third of gator nests.   Average clutch:
of 38 eggs   24 hatchlings emerge. 10 will

live 1 year   & of these yearlings 8 become
subadults (4 ft in length).   Approximately 5

reach maturity.   & I may be no good   at math
but my years of sobriety say   that's a fighting chance.

FROM GRANNY LULA'S DIARY

Jan. 2, 1938: Went to church. In afternoon, Dad, Tom, Archie went [on] motorcycle rides.

April 22, 1938: I went to Mary's finished making my wedding dress pressed everything of Mike's & some of Daddy's clothes. The day of days. Mike came & we ate then we went to Tampa. We were married just before 3 o'clock. We stopped by the monument & Dad & Mike got beer & I a Coca Cola. Mike kissed me then. We came over the Causeway & left Daddy in town.

May 29, 1938: Got up late & killed chicken.

June 8, 1938: I washed.

Nov. 5, 1938: Mike helped load hogs Leroy sold. I ironed.

April 22, 1939: Our anniversary, but we didn't celebrate it very much.

May 27, 1939: I had a crink in my neck.

Sept. 20, 1939: We went to Anice's to milk cows.

Oct. 5, 1939: I didn't feel good at all, but I did my work.

Oct. 18, 1939: Rainy. Mike went to work but came home at noon. We fooled around.

Oct. 20, 1941: Mike's birthday. Daddy ate dinner & supper with us. We had fried chicken & birthday cake.

FLORIDA MAN (A SELF-PORTRAIT)

I'd usually make a joke: weird stuff happens
everywhere, you just hear about it more in Florida

because we have sun, saltwater, & drugs
lots & lots of drugs. But now, I have something

different to tell. In the Gulf of Mexico, ancient
mangroves – walking trees – are survivors.

Their deep root systems filter & provide shelter
to bright fish & corals. As a child, I played in their

legs & stepped on a sea urchin. My blood mixed
with saltwater & sand. I later swam with dolphins

manatees & nurse sharks: give birth to live
young about 20-50 pups. I collected sand dollars

with my toes & could identify shells: turkey wings,
coquina, keyhole limpets (we called pyramids).

I felt the push of an undertow: current moves
offshore as waves approach. It can drag people

out to sea like a message in a bottle. Don't fight
this current. Swim in the direction of the shoreline.

I'd remember this handy wisdom decades later
when a friend & I were out in water far from beach

towels & cooler snacks. She started to panic.
I helped guide her. Juan Ponce de León documented

this peninsula in the early 1500s, but people lived here
long before he tried to find the Fountain of Youth.

To become forever young, visit plastic surgeons
in Miami & while you're there look to Cuba, remember

those who fled Castro's regime. The city's beaches
were submerged, once. Scientists say it'll happen again

if we don't stop what we're doing soon & of course
we won't. Years ago, a boy drove me through oranges –

our state symbol on license plates. Grove stretched
to a late-night horizon between Tampa & Orlando.

Orange groves homesteaded in the early 1900s
as neat rows. Now, their acres have shrunk like old

men. They've been thinned by the Asian citrus
psyllid which carries bacteria, attacks, vascular

system & kills trees, plus hurricanes & freezes
have devastated the crops. Their production down

over 60 percent since the year I thought I left
Florida & all the state's stories behind me.

HEAT

I

096 a million years ago mermaids walked on land
097 hot girl summer sonnet
098 the sky is so god damn beautiful
099 i didn't want to write another political poem
101 is that a banana in your pocket or are you just happy
102 sonnet for the forgotten mermaids
103 hot girl summer bingo card
104 sounds of alligator mating season at big cypress
105 a fighting chance
106 summer afternoon in fl pt. 2
107 thousands in florida sign up to shoot guns at hurricane

ADVISORY

II

i want to write happy poems about florida, but at times our relationship is   **110**

dear families the florida state board of education recently created a new rule (voicemail, 2023)   **111**

a poem for pride as it gets cancelled in some florida cities (2023)   **112**

portrait w/ *creature from the black lagoon* (filmed in florida, 1954)   **114**

the sky is gay. i don't make the rules   **116**

hitching wagons to stars (found poem, 1928)   **117**

i'm in miami, beach!   **118**

heat advisory   **119**

on a day i'm feeling especially bummed out about florida   **120**

I

A MILLION YEARS AGO MERMAIDS WALKED ON LAND

then their feet   turned to flippers. Dove
headfirst into water.   Found pastures

of turtle grass   mangrove leaves & hydrilla.
Mermaids took to water.   But they still craved

sky *of deities*   *or mortals*   *or of both.*

Christopher Columbus   saw mermaids
– now called manatees –   rise from the sea.

He noted they weren't as "pretty" as the painters imagined.

HOT GIRL SUMMER SONNET

for Tombolo Books in Saint Petersburg

I sit with witches & other poets   in a Pentagram.
We're pouring over birth charts   when a breeze
snuffs incense   someone brought to the bookstore
as a gift.   This time last year   I was more depressed

than ever. Now, I'm still   depressed but in a sexy
way.   I wear tight blue jeans   & twirl my hair
around tattooed artists   emotionally in retrograde.
Freud posits   anxiety stems from a conscious

suppression   of dangerous feelings while Megan
Thee Stallion argues   *bad b*tches*   *have bad*
days, too.   I'm wary of psychoanalysis
but see merit in the doctrine   of real hot girl sh*t.

See merit in being   with people who will turn
their eyes to stars   then howl with you at the moon.

THE SKY IS SO GOD DAMN BEAUTIFUL

Before another hurricane in FL our sky oranges into baby blue and blushes pink. Distracts us from a coming storm named Idalia. One of my students mishears this name as dahlia like the flower. He suggests we stop naming hurricanes after people because it makes them seem nonthreatening. Says *let's call them Death and Destruction or Serial Killer Storms.* The college cancels classes in the middle of mine. I buy underwear on my way home. I always thought the sky looks blue because it reflects water. Science laughs at my independent research. When will we be safe? I ask. Science gets quiet. I'm trying to write a Hopeful poem in this silence. I want to conjure sunny days, but all I can do is stare into the blue-black.

I DIDN'T WANT TO WRITE ANOTHER
POLITICAL POEM

but then Florida banned bodies   banned books

politicians hadn't read   banned things we can think
& say   a gay man who's taught in the same FL school

for decades told me   *it's just too much.* I didn't want

to write another   political poem about power & men
who have it. Instead, I wanted to write   about the moon

as a metaphor for queer love.   I wanted to have a hot
girl summer & write about how sexy   I find punctuation.

My desire to cuddle with ethically non-monogamous question marks.

Allen Ginsberg howled   it's the job of the poet to keep
people up at night   thinking.   Florida, of course, banned

him & the beat poets in the 60s   called them the downfall

of American literature.   Sound familiar? Poems they haven't
read help us understand ourselves, each other   & power doesn't

want that.   Some theorists argue all poems are political
on the aesthetic level. Poetry plays with line   breaks ideas

of grammar   & logic & forms   its own conclusions.
I don't know if I agree with those theorists, but I do know Florida

is my home & this poem cannot sit in silence   so I stand with banned
books & bodies & teachers   & anyone who thinks   *it's just too much.*

I mean   we may not all agree   on poetry's function
but most of us are tired   of powers who say they don't get

our lines   when they haven't even tried   to read them.

IS THAT A BANANA IN YOUR POCKET
OR ARE YOU JUST HAPPY

SONNET FOR THE FORGOTTEN MERMAIDS

In the 1970s, Jacques Cousteau visited Florida
to film *The Forgotten Mermaids*. By then, manatees
made the Sunshine State home. They migrate south
to St. John's River with "first cold breath of autumn."

Warm-blooded aquatic mammals survive here
because "although they look fat, they do not have
much of an insulating layer." Cousteau watched
these myths in blue springs. Described the state

as littered with cars: "monuments of man's carelessness."
He noted "chaotic development drained & destroyed"
our state's natural resources & Oh! If only he could see it
now: mermaids entangled in ropes & lines & nets.

They're hit by boats, barges. Gauged. Crushed in flood
gates & pipes. They drown when can't reach the sky.

HOT GIRL SUMMER BINGO CARD

written at the beginning of summer with Kate Walker

Reject an ex
Date someone from high school
Vacation hookup
Bag a tourist
Quit your job
Play hooky from work
Kiss a coworker
Skinny dip
Smoke a joint
Make pot brownie
Send a sexy pic (consensually)
Go to church
Play spin the bottle
Get a wax job
Twerk
Kiss a stranger
Eat a churro
Lick a popsicle
Have sex on a first date
Jump into the ocean
Skip gym day
Girls' Night Out
Act like a ho
Stay in on a Friday
Binge your favorite TV show
Pet a dog

SOUNDS OF ALLIGATOR MATING SEASON
AT BIG CYPRESS

A FIGHTING CHANCE

If I remember correctly   only about five baby
alligators from each clutch survive   to adulthood.

I can't fact check this info right now.   I'm in a FL swamp

with no service.   Moon guides my path. Finally
reach alligator. Bird hangs   from his mouth.

This bird once lodged   in my throat, too. It made

me sing   such a nasty song. Never imagined my father
would bring me   this peace offering. I'll be honest:

I don't know if we can every truly change.

But I do know tonight.   We've survived our nature
this long   & I'm grateful the universe gave us

a fighting chance & we can at least try   to figure out our sh*t.

SUMMER AFTERNOON IN FL PT. 2

just stay inside

THOUSANDS IN FLORIDA SIGN UP TO SHOOT GUNS AT HURRICANE

Birds hear the storm first   & leave.
A friend texts I can   go to Mississippi

if I need. Decide to stand my ground. This time.

Mom worries about morning   waitress
shifts. Can't afford   to miss work. My brother
obsessively tracks it. Suggests we move

to Canada. I stop writing   this poem

& help my stepdad put up shutters. Watch traffic
light near our street   blink red, blind red.

Wind tells us it's time   to go inside. It rains.

& rains & rains   until I can't see the street
light anymore. The house tries   to sleep.
I creep out back.   Take off my shirt.

Extend middle finger   to the sky

then pair it with pointer. Cock hand
to clouds. Yell   into its demon mouth.

I shoot at the hurricane   because
nothing else   drowns out this noise.

Real Florida "Poetry"

For some unexplained reason, the poetic output in Florida this season has been pitifully small. Usually, the tourist season develops one hundred or more merry rhymesters, both local and imported, who sing the beauties of our streams and woods, our fruits and flowers, our birds and beasts (human included); and their home-papers as well as the Florida papers are compelled at the risk of serious losses of subscribers and friends, to devote much space to the presentation of these immortelles in indestructible type.

The past winter, however, we have had a dearth of poets. Whether our visitors have been too busy enjoying life and our fellow-citizens too busy entertaining them, or whether there has been a lack of inspiration, it is not for the Tribune to say. But, speaking from our own experience, our poetry column and our poetry wastbasket have been alike most unusually empty throughout the festive period.

II

I WANT TO WRITE HAPPY POEMS ABOUT FLORIDA, BUT AT TIMES OUR RELATIONSHIP IS

toxic   red tide, report: 554 manatees
died   as 267 tons of marine life

washed up on   Florida's Gulf Coast.

Scientists blamed heavy rainfall   ocean
temperature   wind patterns   & pollution

paired with simultaneous   freshwater bloom.

Organisms   in blue-green algae
turned mutant slime   from regulatory issues.

Governor declared state   of emergency.
Same governor took a half million   from Big Sugar

& the sea – our oldest historian – won't forget any of it.

DEAR FAMILIES THE FLORIDA STATE
BOARD OF EDUCATION RECENTLY CREATED
A NEW RULE (VOICEMAIL, 2023)

A POEM FOR PRIDE AS IT GETS CANCELLED IN SOME FLORIDA CITIES (2023)

We crawled from the ocean   to get to this beach
then argued   over who can sit on its sand.

I mean, I may not know much   about science
but weren't we all in the same primordial goo?

Didn't we all adapt   to land & language?
I never learned those details.   Southern Baptists

taught me God made humans   & there'd be more
moondust if science   were true.   Animals like me

went to hell for doing what we do.   I tried to change.
Pressed my ear to shell.   Only heard you. A million years

passed: the storm is nothing new.   At first, this poem thought
it would trace Florida's homophobia from the Johns Committee

in the 1950s   to Anita Bryant's campaign in the 70s to now.
This poem thought   it would make a political statement

about history & book bans & fascism & saying gay & voting
& civil liberties & trans youth & safety concerns & healthcare

& LGBTQ+ elders & the government   & demanding change.
This poem thought it would be political   but deep down

it felt the thumpa thumpa music of a parade   so it put on
lipstick, eyelashes   a dress & a wig then shimmied

into the sea   of Pinellas Queens & Floridians who want
to clean up the red tide.   This poem danced all day.

Got sweaty   flirted & even consensually made out
with another poem who understood   its form.

Pride helped this poem realize   we will withstand
these waves   & our joy   is a resistance itself.

PORTRAIT W/ *CREATURE FROM THE BLACK LAGOON* (1954, FILMED IN FLORIDA)

The men don't shoot the creature in this ending.
Instead, Gill-Man becomes friends with Kay,

the movie's other star. They drink mimosas,
decide to go on a road trip. Pack an electric

car & drive around Florida. They talk art & poetry
at charging stations. Roadside blurs into sunset.

Gill-Man booked nights at Wakulla Springs
where he filmed. His turtle friends tell him

the water isn't as clear as when you were here.
Urge him to be the spring's voice. He says, he tried

but men put him in a cage. Reminds them he's more
than a climate change metaphor. He & Kay play

boardgames in the lodge & listen to Loretta Lynn sing
about fighting her man's mistress. They later apply

expensive lotion before bed & discuss how bitter
sweet it is to be an adult. After their trip, they share

memes. Kay tells him *there's a guy you should meet.*
She sets him up with me. Of course, he's my type –

beautiful, mysterious, complicated. Friends urge
the creature's home is the water & yours is the sky.

I respond: the creature has a name – it's Gill-Man.
I learn how to breathe underwater. Use some sticks

& mud to make a home. I grill seaweed after work.
Rub his claws. He laughs at my jokes. The future

happens. Our stick home withstands the waves.
Our love is ours. That's all we ever wanted it to be.

THE SKY IS GAY. I DON'T MAKE THE RULES

Muse, o muse! The thunder cracks   & I know
you're here: in Florida   the lightning capital. Bolts

blaze this day something fierce   as *heat expands*
the air around it   *& creates a shockwave.*   We hear

boom.   I learn this science from a cereal box.
There's poetry   everywhere. It heats   our words until

Boom!   A caesura.   O muse!   This state of shells

is shambles.   I'm worried about alliteration   in their patterns.
But right now, I'm emotional   about clouds.   Can't get over

the fact they're constantly changing.   Ice crystals of abstract art

we can look at whenever   we want.   Don't tell me there's no
god.   Don't tell me   aliens aren't real. Mars has clouds
like ours   but Jupiter makes clouds ammonia.   I learn this science

from NASA. Based in Florida   they study ice crystals.   After storm

passes   our sky blue-pink-whites   the colors of a trans flag
& later the sun comes out   as a double rainbow.   I pause.

Visual caesura.   There's poetry in my home state's sky.

& we know clouds shift with the wind. But muse!   O muse!
Please remind us this   as we do our best   to syllable a new dawn.

HITCHING WAGONS TO STARS

A Florida man is laying plans for the construction of a giant rocket, in which he hopes to be shot from the earth to the planet Venus.

This is altogether a laudable ambition, even though reports thus far published fail to state just what he expects to do after he gets there or how he thinks he is going to get back. A great many of us, at one time or another, have wanted very much to go sailing off to a distant star.

Indeed, you might say that the yearning to do that is every man's heritage. This is especially true in youth. There are times, particularly, when one is young and easily hurt, when the breaking of illusions is so painful that this earth seems rather a makeshift planet, at best, and the unattainable stars shine very invitingly.

I'M IN MIAMI, BEACH!

At a hotel, I pour milk into iced coffee   & watch galaxies
spiral in glass   then wish I could go back in time

to film it for socials.   Because everything is content

in this new landscape. I'm by myself   on South Beach.
Can see famous sand   as I eat Cuban molletes outside
with smokers – the only other people   who'll take bites

of this heat.   A fitness model runs by us & Death follows

on rollerblades.   How much Life do you spend thinking
about mortality?   I'm sure it's a lot.   You're a poet.

The smokers near me sip fruit juice   & give pocket change
to someone who asks.   Death shoots me   a thumbs up.

Night before we'd been making out on a dancefloor.
It's awkward, but I wave back.   Sunshine makes me

somewhat forgiving of a f*ckboy   in dark robes
that somehow don't get caught in his skates. Death stops
trailing the model.   Makes his way toward the smokers.

& me: I still think Life   is all about having your heart

broken   as many times as you can   & tasting as much
new fruit as possible with a sunset   on your face.

HEAT ADVISORY

That summer we spent all our time
small talking weather.　　Only said

it's so hot　　&　　*it's scorching outside.*

Didn't discuss philosophy　　or art
or process　　the sadness of having no
children of our own.　　Weatherman called it

a streak of record highs:　　nine years & counting.

I canceled all my plans.　　Didn't fall in love
even once.　　Only had the briefest of flings

with an artist.　　He left town before we kissed.

I missed　　all my deadlines　　& blamed it
on global warming.　　That summer was too hot

to have sex, anyway.　　Sweat pooled in gross
places I won't mention.　　Couldn't body another

stomach on mine. Fall came　　& I began to wonder
if it truly had been that scorching　　or maybe

I've just reached a Time　　when I notice my mortality

in mirrors. Weatherman said　　only luck will bring more gray
storms in your beard. Told me　　you better get used to the heat.

ON A DAY I'M FEELING ESPECIALLY BUMMED OUT ABOUT FLORIDA

I'm late for work & stuck
in bridge traffic when I spot
a hawk overhead with silver
lining clutched in talons.

Bird flaps sailboat winds
as fish pulses final minutes
in horizon full of sherbet:
orange cream & strawberry

delight. They disappear in jewel
water – my favorite color: sand
reaching from ocean to touch sky.
Corner of my eye, dolphin breaks

surface & in this moment I swear
I see God. Traffic finally moves.

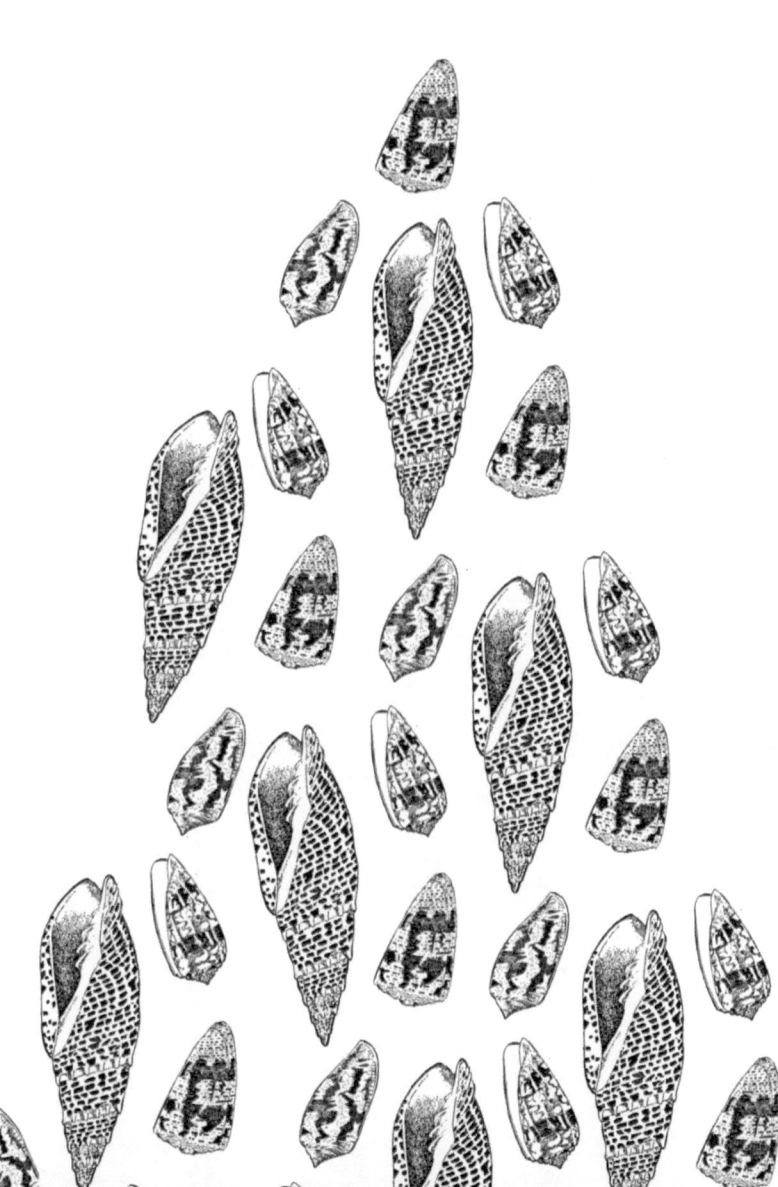

ABOUT THE AUTHOR

Tyler Gillespie is an award-winning educator and writer whose work has appeared in the *New Yorker*, *Rolling Stone*, *GQ*, *The Guardian*, *The Washington Post*, *Playboy*, and elsewhere. He's the author of the nonfiction collection *The Thing about Florida: Exploring a Misunderstood State* (University Press of Florida) and two poetry collections *Florida Man: Poems* and *the nature machine!* (Autofocus).

RESEARCH NOTES AND REFERENCES FOR *FLORIDA MAN: POEMS, REVISITED*

a florida man has an alligator farm compiled headlines form archived newspapers:
"A Florida Man Has an Alligator Farm," *Butler County Democrat*, Jul 12, 1883.
"Radium Cures Cancer in Throat of Florida Man," *Chattanooga Daily Times*, Jun 01, 1914.
"Finds Fiancée After Three-Year Chase," *Oakland Tribune*, Sep 12, 1912.
"Missing Thirty Years," *Chattanooga Daily Times*, Jan 25, 1913.
"For Sale," *The Evansville Journal*, Sep 19, 1913.
"Collects $1,000 – Then Faints," *The Mexia Weekly Herald*, Mar 25, 1948.
"The Florida man," *Corsicana Weekly Light*, Apr 03, 1975.

Alligator Tears
quotes *The Travels of Sir John Mandeville: The Version of the Cotton Manuscript in Modern Spelling*. Project Gutenberg (e-book), p.190.

consults interview with Tim Williams at Gatorland in Orlando, FL.

consults University of Florida. (2007, October 3). Researchers: No Faking It, Crocodile Tears Are Real. Retrieved from http://news.ufl.edu/archive/2007/10/researchers-no-faking-it-crocodile-tears-are-real.php

Bush v Gore Election, 2000
quotes Bill Maher from the article "COUNTING THE VOTE: HUMOR; Television Shows Find Comedy in the Errors." Scott, Janny. (2000, Nov. 17). *New York Times*. Retrieved from https://www.nytimes.com/2000/11/17/us/counting-the-vote-humor-television-shows-find-comedy-in-the-errors.html

quotes Deborah Clark conversation at the University of South Florida-St. Petersburg.

Florida Man
quotes Kenneth Krysko from the article "Killer Nile crocodiles in Florida? Experts say it's possible." Spencer, Terry. Associated Press, referenced in Fox 13 newscast. Retrieved from http://www.fox13news.com/news/florida-news/killer-nile-crocodiles-in-florida-

Year of Headlines on @_FloridaMan Twitter Account (381,000 Followers)
Lingan, John. (2016, June 21). America's Long, Rich History of Trashing Poor Whites. *Pacific Standard*. Retrieved from https://psmag.com/news/americas-long-rich-history-of-trashing-poor-whites

quotes @_FloridaMan. (from 11 April 2016 to 7 April 2017). Twitter.

A Second-Generation Alligator Wrestler
quotes Clint Bridges interview at Everglades Holiday Park.

poetry, at last! reproduces text found in "Poetry, at Last!," *The Tampa Tribune*, June 28, 1910.

None in the Wild are Native
consults Casler, Michelle L, Mazzotti, Frank, & Taylor, Amy K. (1993). Parrots and Parakeets in Florida, a WEC-XXX document, one of a series of the Department of Wildlife.

Landscape in Which Alligator Fights Python
quotes WILX Staff. (2018, Jan. 16). Python wraps itself around alligator. WILX. Retrieved from http://www.wilx.com/content/news/Python-wraps-itself-around-alligator-469511253.html

Florida Woman Repeatedly Slapped Grandma for Rejecting Facebook Friend Request
consults Zennie, Michael. (2014, Dec. 19). Face slap over Facebook: Woman, 27, arrested for smacking her own GRANDMOTHER, age 72, after she rejected her friend request. *Daily Mail.* Retrieved from http://www.dailymail.co.uk/news/article-2880831/Face-slap-Facebook-Woman-27-arrested-smacking-GRANDMOTHER-age-72-rejected-friend-request.html

quotes Rachel Hayes interview in Fort Lauderdale, FL.

consults Schiltz, James Joseph. Time to grow up: The rise and fall of spring break in Fort Lauderdale. Diss. Iowa State University, 2013. Web.

quotes Catherine Cameron interview at Stetson University College of Law.

capture of a desperado compiled headlines form archived newspapers:
"Capture of a Desperado," *Chicago Tribune*, April 09, 1884.
"Whipped by Women," *The San Francisco Call*, April 29, 1895
"Bigamist Arrested," *Chattanooga Daily Times*, Oct. 09, 1905.
"Florida Man Bound Over on Prohibition Charge," *The Atlanta Journal*, April 16, 1921.
"Florida Man Arrested as He Leaves Jail," *The Times Leader*, Sept. 02, 1961
"Return of Florida Man in City Death Uncertain," *Albuquerque Journal*, Sept. 25, 1975.
"Drunken, naked man fired weapons, police say," *The Index-Journal*, Oct. 05, 2017.

What Is Up with Florida
consults Associated Press. (2017, Jan. 25). Foster child, 14, hangs herself while using Facebook Live. NBC 2. Retrieved from http://www.nbc-2.com/story/34341795/foster-child-14-hangs-herself-while-using-facebook-live

quotes Donald Trump from 2004 interview with Don Imus replayed on The Daily Show with Trevor Noah. Retrieved from http://www.cc.com/video-clips/kqdjut/the-daily-show-with-trevor-noah-donald-trump-s-long-history-of-sexism.

quotes John Fitzgibbons from the article "Too pretty for prison" by Suzanne Goldenberg. (2006, Mar. 23). *The Guardian*. Retrieved from https://www.theguardian.com/world/2006/mar/24/usa.gender

Gator Clan
quotes Billy Walker interview recorded by Sofia Valiente in Hollywood, FL.

Gas Station Gator Head
quotes Robert McDade from the article "Need an Alligator Head? This Guy Can Hook You Up" by Leigh Buchanan. (2015, Mar. 10). *Inc. magazine*. Retrieved from https://www.inc.com/leigh-buchanan/need-an-alligator-head-this-guy-can-hook-you-up.html

Alligator facts from the Florida Fish and Wildlife Conservation Commission website (myfwc.com).

RESEARCH NOTES AND REFERENCES FOR *HEAT ADVISORY*

a million years ago mermaids walked on land borrows the line "of deities or mortals, or of both" from "Ode on a Grecian Urn" by John Keats.

sonnet for the forgotten mermaids borrows lines from episodes of *The Forgotten Mermaids*, 1972.

sounds of alligator mating season at big cypress from "Love is in the Air! Sights & Sounds of Alligator Mating Season at Big Cypress. YouTube, uploaded by Big Cypress NPS, 10 Aug. 2012, https://www.youtube.com/watch?v=AmhXTHigl2E&ab_channel=BigCypressNPS

thousands in florida sign up to shoot guns at hurricane borrows its title from a *GQ* article

real florida poetry reproduces text found in "Real Florida Poetry," *The Tampa Tribune*, April 2, 1913.

dear families the florida state board of education recently created a new rule (voicemail, 2023) from Polk County Public Schools.

the sky is gay. i don't make the rules references information on the box for Wonderworks Keto Friendly Chocolate Cereal.

hitching wagons to stars (found poem, 1928) reproduces text found in *The Selma Times-Journal*, Jan 29, 1928.

ACKNOWLEDGMENTS

Many thanks to the readers and editors of the following journals in which these poems previously appeared:
Cleaver: "Florida Man"
Creative Loafing: "i didn't want to write another political poem"
Flyway: Journal of Writing & Environment: "Gas Station Gator Head" and "Alligator Mississippiens"
St. Pete Pride Guide: "a poem for pride as it gets cancelled in some florida cities (2023)"
The Journal: "Alligator Tears"

Thanks to editors of the following publications in which parts of the reporting previously appeared in a different form:

VICE: "Disney May Rule, But Gator Wrestling and Roadside Attractions Remain in Florida"
Salon: "The Florida woman trying to break free of being 'Florida Woman'"

My gratitude to Ryan Rivas at Burrow Press for all his work on this edition and Michael Burk who designed the cover.

Randy Bates, Carolyn Hembree, Keith O'Brien, Robert Hooker, Martha Brenckle, Dahlia El-Shafei, Florentina Staigers, Phyllis Dunham, Wren Hanks, Clare Harmon, Jessie Strauss, Jade Hurter, Jessica Morey-Collins, Laurin Dechae, Jessica Smith, Rev Miranda, Bryan Borland, my agent Lauren MacLeod, and all the Floridians who spent time with me for this project.

I'm also grateful for the support of the University of New Orleans Creative Writing Workshop, University of South Florida, the Salon Young Americans fellowship, and The Writer's Room at The Besty.

www.ingramcontent.com/pod-product-compliance
Lightning Source LLC
Chambersburg PA
CBHW060531080526
44586CB00012B/700